W9-AVK-148

BIG SNAKES

HUNTERS OF THE NIGHT

Elaine Landau

WORDS TO KNOW

camouflage— Coloring that helps something hide in its surroundings.

endangered—In danger of dying out.

Jacobson's organ— An organ in a snake that can sense some chemicals released by a nearby animal.

mating—The way animals have babies.

predators—Animals that eat other animals for food.

prey—Animals that are eaten by other animals.

scales—The very small hard pieces that cover a snake's body.

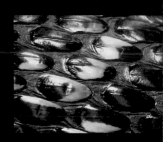

symbol—Something that stands for something else.

venom—A poison made by an animal.

venomous—Poisonous.

CONTENTS

This rattlesnake
is ready to strike.

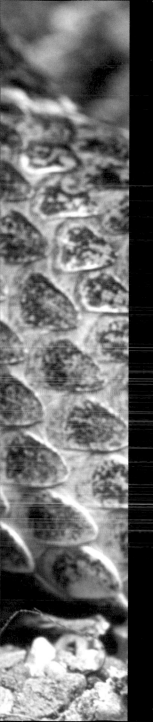

AFTER DARK IN THE DESERT

It is a hot summer night. The desert is quiet. Yet, some animals are awake. Among them is a large, hungry rattlesnake.

The snake is on the path. It has been there for hours. It is waiting for a meal.

Finally, a big rat comes along. The rattlesnake strikes! Its fangs send venom, or poison, into the rat. The rat moves away but does not get far. The venom is killing it.

Now the rattler opens its jaws very wide and swallows the rat whole. This rattlesnake will not be hungry for a week.

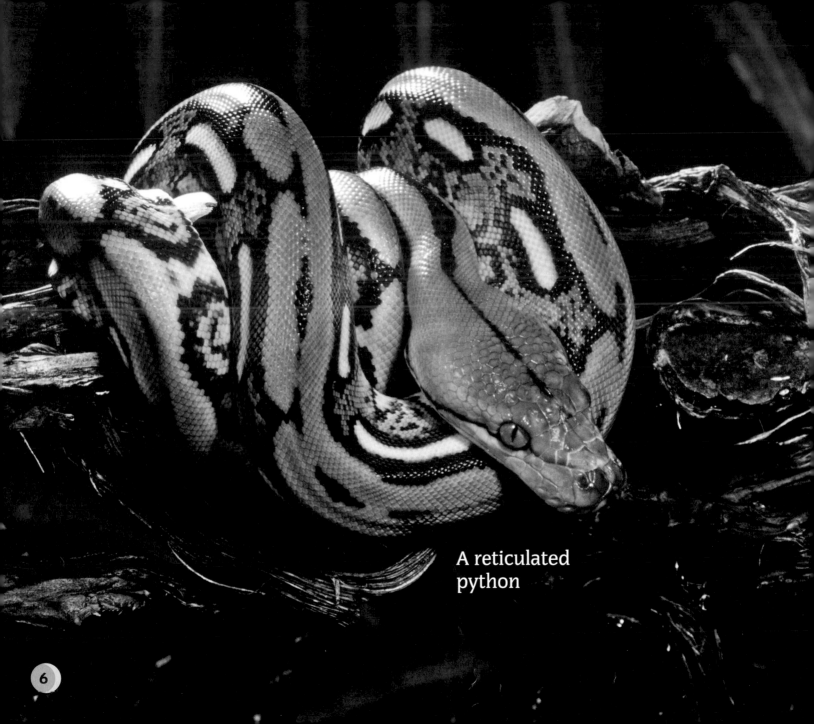

A reticulated
python

MEET THE BIG SNAKES

There are almost three thousand types of snakes in the world. Some are venomous (VEN-um-us), or poisonous, though most snakes are not.

Some snakes are small, while others are very large. The reticulated (reh-TIH-kyoo-lay-ted) python can grow to more than forty-five feet long. That is the length of a bus! The green anaconda can weigh over four hundred pounds!

Snakes do not have arms, legs, or wings. Snakes also have scales on their skin. A snake's scales might look slimy, but they are really dry.

Snakes are reptiles. They are related to other reptiles like crocodiles, turtles, and lizards.

Like all reptiles, a snake's body temperature changes with its surroundings. On a cool day, a snake will rest in the sun. Its body will soon warm up. A snake that wants to cool off will crawl under a bush or rock.

Like people, snakes have skeletons. But a snake's skeleton only has a head and a long backbone. Some snakes can twist themselves around objects. Many snakes can slip through narrow spaces or move into small holes.

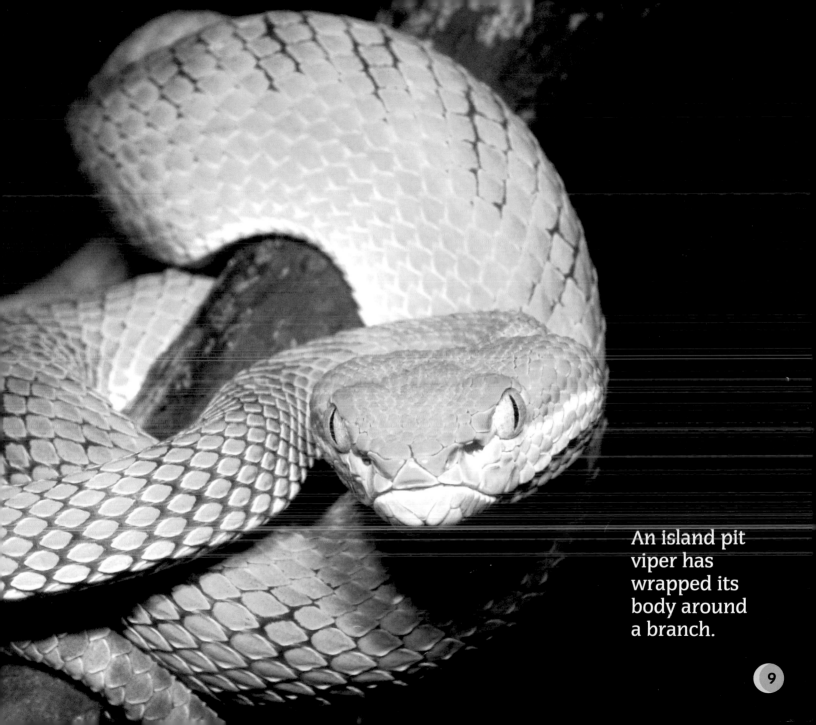

An island pit viper has wrapped its body around a branch.

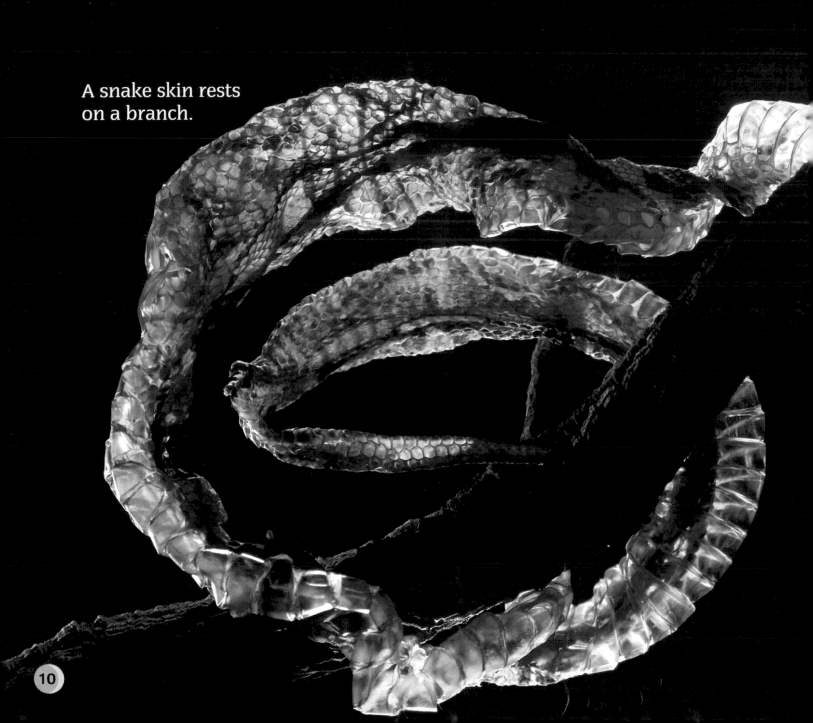

A snake skin rests on a branch.

SNAKES THROUGH HISTORY

Snakes have been on Earth for about 100 million years. Scientists believe that they descended, or came from, lizards. Over time, they lost their arms and legs.

Snakes have been both feared and praised by people. The ancient Greek god of healing carried a walking stick with a snake carved on it. Today, a walking stick with a snake around it is a symbol of healing.

Some people see snakes as a sign of new life. This is because snakes shed their old skins for new ones.

NIGHT HUNTING

Snakes are good night hunters. They do not use sight and hearing the way people do. A snake uses other senses instead.

A snake has a forked, or split, tongue. The snake flicks out its tongue. When its tongue goes back into its mouth, it touches the snake's Jacobson's organ. This organ, or body part, senses the taste and smell of a nearby animal. It lets the snake know that a meal is close.

Snakes also use nostrils to pick up stronger scents and those coming from far away. Snakes sometimes place their jaws on the ground to feel the other animals' movements as well.

Some snakes, such as pit vipers, have special organs for hunting after dark. These are pits on each side of the snake's head that sense the heat of prey.

This white-lipped viper's pits are above its mouth. The viper shows its forked tongue, too.

A boa constrictor kills a mouse by squeezing it. Then, it swallows the mouse whole.

Snakes are meat eaters. They eat mice, rats, birds, frogs, turtles, rabbits, pigs, small deer, other snakes, and other animals. Big snakes eat big animals.

Sometimes, snakes quietly sneak up on their prey. Other times, they wait for them. Often they will stay near an animal trail. Prey is likely to pass there. They will wait in the same spot for days.

Venomous snakes like mambas and cobras use their deadly venom to kill the animals they eat. Constrictor snakes, such as boas and pythons, wrap their bodies around their prey. The animal cannot breathe and dies.

A snake does not chew its food. It swallows its prey whole. The lower jaw of a snake's mouth opens very wide. A snake can eat animals that are larger than its head!

The snake's strong jaw and throat muscles push the food into its stomach. Depending on the size of the prey, the snake needs between a few days and more than a week to digest it.

WHERE THE BIG SNAKES ARE

Most big snakes live where the weather is warm. They are found in fields and forests, on rocky hillsides, underground, and in wetlands.

Cottonmouth snakes are mostly found in wetlands in the southeastern United States. Other big snakes live in grasslands and deserts. Rattlesnakes live in deserts and forests from Canada to South America. Many are in the United States.

Still other snakes live in trees, caves, or in fresh or salt water. Many boa constrictors are good climbers. They are often spotted in rain forests. In some places, snakes are also found in towns and cities.

The cottonmouth snake spends time in the water. Cottonmouths are also called water moccasins.

STAYING ALIVE

The color and design of a snake's scales help it stay alive. Brown or grayish rattlesnakes match the ground and rocks. Copperhead snakes have wide reddish-brown bands to match logs. Predators cannot easily see them. This is known as **camouflage**.

Poisonous snakes are often brightly colored. Their bright colors warn **predators** to stay away. Other snakes scare off predators by lifting their heads up high or thrashing about. When a cobra is angry, a piece of loose skin called a **hood** flares out behind its head.

Snakes also use sounds as a defense. Some snakes hiss. Rattlesnakes shake rattles at the ends of their tails.

Still other snakes break off a tail if a predator has grabbed it. A new tail grows back to replace it.

This copperhead is the same
color as the log it is on.

A baby green mamba breaks out of its egg.

RAISING YOUNG

At mating time, a female snake gives off a special scent so the male can find her. Most female snakes lay from six to thirty eggs a few weeks after mating. These hatch in six to twelve weeks. Female snakes do not usually stay with their eggs until they hatch. However, some types of female snakes stay to protect their eggs from predators.

Other snakes give birth to live young. Among these are rattlesnakes and garter snakes. The first year of a young snake's life is very dangerous. Many are eaten by crows, skunks, snapping turtles, baboons, and other animals, including other snakes.

HOW SNAKES MOVE

Snakes do not have legs or feet. Yet they move with ease. Here are the three main ways snakes move:

The S-shaped Wave

Here the snake uses its muscles to curve its body. It looks something like the letter S. The curves of the snake's body push against the ground. This moves the snake forward in a wavy path.

The Belly Crawl

Larger, heavier snakes move this way. These snakes push down on their belly scales and slide forward. They move ahead in a nearly straight line.

Side Winding

Snakes that live on sand move this way. To move forward, the snake lifts the main part of its body and thrusts it forward sideways. Then it moves its head and tail up to the rest of its body. The sidewinder rattlesnake moves this way.

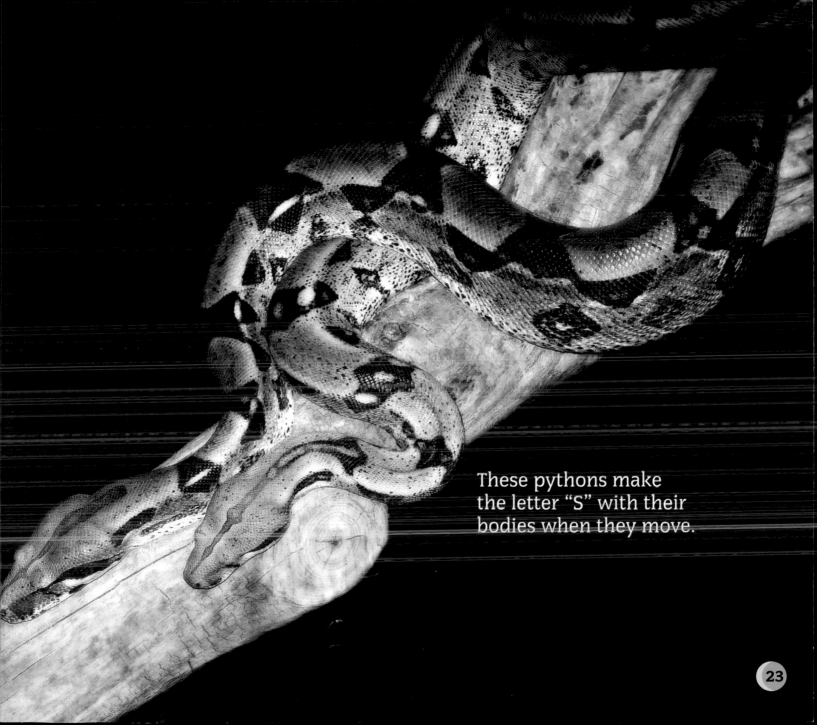

These pythons make the letter "S" with their bodies when they move.

SNAKES AND PEOPLE

Though only a small number of snakes are dangerous, many people are afraid of snakes. Some people have killed snakes out of fear.

Snakes have been killed for other reasons too. In some places, people eat snakes. Snakes have often been killed for their skins. Some people like to own snakeskin purses, belts, and boots.

Snakes also die when the places they live are changed. Forests have been cleared and swamps drained to make way for farms and towns. This happened to the eastern indigo snake—the biggest snake in the United States. Many of the places where it lives in the Southeast have been changed. Now there are fewer of these snakes left.

These kids are holding a really big snake! Some snakes are dangerous. Kids should not touch snakes unless an adult they know and trust says it is okay.

THE FUTURE

Some snakes in the world are endangered, or in danger of dying out. Laws have been passed so that endangered snakes cannot be killed, collected, or sold.

At this time, there are no endangered snakes in the United States. But some big snakes are threatened. This means that they could become endangered. These include the eastern indigo snake and the concho water snake. Threatened snakes are also protected by law.

Snakes are more useful than you may know. Big snakes eat rats and mice that destroy farm crops. Snakes are a part of nature. It is important that they be here in the future.

The indigo snake is seen less and less as the places it lives in are changed by people.

An Indian cobra shows its hood.

FUN FACTS ABOUT BIG SNAKES

★ A cobra's biggest enemy is the mongoose. A mongoose  is only about sixteen inches long but is very fast. When it attacks a cobra, it almost always kills it.

★ The oldest snake in a zoo was a boa constrictor named Popeye from the Philadelphia Zoo. It lived for more than forty years.

★ The biggest snake ever captured is a forty-nine-foot python. It is on display at a park in Indonesia.

★ Wearing boots that cover the ankle could stop about 25 percent of all snakebites.

★ Snake teeth usually point backward toward its throat. That keeps a snake's prey from getting away.

TO KNOW MORE ABOUT BIG SNAKES

BOOKS:

Hernandez-Divers, Sonia. *Snakes.* Chicago: Heinemann Library, 2003.

Landau, Elaine. *Sinister Snakes.* Berkeley Heights, N.J.: Enslow Publishers, 2003.

Richardson, Adele. *Mambas.* Mankato, Minn.: Capstone, 2004.

Taylor, Barbara. *Cobras.* Austin, Tex.: Raintree Steck-Vaughn Publishers, 2003.

INTERNET ADDRESSES:

Cobra Information Site

See this Web site for lots of great facts on cobras. There are wonderful pictures, too.

<http://www.cobras.org>

Rattlesnakes

Visit this site for some great fun facts on rattlesnakes.

<http://www.sandiegozoo.org/ animalbytes/t-rattlesnake.html>

INDEX

Enslow Elementary, an imprint of Enslow Publishers, Inc.

Enslow Elementary® is a registered trademark of Enslow Publishers, Inc.

Library of Congress Cataloging-in-Publication Data

Landau, Elaine.
    Big snakes : hunters of the night / Elaine Landau.
        p. cm. — (Animals after dark)
    Includes bibliographical references and index.
    ISBN-13: 978-0-7660-2769-5
    ISBN-10: 0-7660-2769-4
    1. Snakes—Juvenile literature. I. Title.
QL666.O6L322 2007
597.96—dc22   2006026517

Printed in the United States of America

10 9 8 7 6 5 4 3 2

To Our Readers: We have done our best to make sure all Internet Addresses in this book were active and appropriate when we went to press. However, the author and the publisher have no control over and assume no liability for the material available on those Internet sites or on other Web sites they may link to. Any comments or suggestions can be sent by e-mail to comments@enslow.com or to the address on the back cover.

Series Literacy Advisor: Dr. Allan A. De Fina, Department of Literacy Education, New Jersey City University.

Illustration Credits: Anthony Bannister/Photo Researchers, Inc., pp. 20–21; Associated Press, pp. 24–25; Clipart.com, p. 11 (right); Dante Fenolio/ Photo Researchers, Inc., pp. 8–9; Heidi Hans-Jurgen Koch/Minden Pictures, pp. 10–11; Jack Milchanowski/Visuals Unlimited, pp. 18–19; Joe McDonald/Visuals Unlimited, pp. 6–7, 16–17, 28; John Serrao/ Photo Researchers, Inc., pp. 26–27; © 2006 Jupiterimages Corporation, pp. 1, 2, 3, 29, 32; McDonald, Joe/Animals Animals–Earth Scenes, pp. 4–5; NHPA/Daniel Heuclin, pp. 23–13; Paul Whitten/Photo Researchers, Inc., p. 14; Sascha Burkard/Shutterstock, pp. 22–23.

Cover Illustration: © 2006 Jupiterimages Corporation (front and back).

Enslow Elementary
an imprint of

Enslow Publishers, Inc.
40 Industrial Road
Box 398
Berkeley Heights, NJ 07922
USA

http://www.enslow.com